D0459154

Swimming

Kirk Bizley

Heinemann Library
Chicago, Illinois

© 2000 Reed Educational & Professional Publishing
Published by Heinemann Library,
an imprint of Reed Educational & Professional Publishing,
100 N. LaSalle, Suite 1010
Chicago, IL 60602

Customer Service 888-454-2279

Designed by Ken Vail Graphic Design
Illustrations by Graham-Cameron Illustration (Susan Hutchinson)
Printed by Wing King Tong in Hong Kong

04 03 02 01 00
10 9 8 7 6 5 4 3 2

Library of Congress Cataloging in Publication Data
Bizley, Kirk.
  Swimming / Kirk Bizley.
      p. cm. – (You can do it!)
  Includes index.
  Summary: An introduction to swimming describing equipment and
strokes, with tips on safety.
  ISBN 1-57572-963-6 (lib. bdg.)
  1. Swimming for children Juvenile literature. [1. Swimming.]
  I. Title. II. Series: You can do it! (Des Plaines, Ill.)
  GV837.2.B54 1999
  797.2'1—dc21   99-22663
                                                            CIP

Acknowledgments
The author would like to thank the staff and students of Shepton Mallett Community Infants School.

The Publishers would like to thank the following for permission to reproduce photographs:
Gareth Boden, pages 4, 10, 14, 16, 20; Empics/Matthew Ashton, page 21; Robert Harding Picture Library/Nigel Francis, page 6.

Cover photograph reproduced with permission of Bubbles /Ian West.

To Chloe

Some words are shown in bold, **like this.** You can find out what they mean by looking in the glossary.

Contents

What Do You Need?

Boys and girls wear swimsuits when they go swimming.

▲ **Chlorine** in the water can make your eyes sore. Goggles will protect your eyes.

▼ **Earplugs** will keep water out of your ears.

▲ You may need to wear a bathing cap, especially if you have long hair.

◀**Water wings** filled with air help you to swim. You wear them on your arms. Let some of the air out as you become a better swimmer.

▶**Kickboards** help you to float in the water. They also help you to use your legs and feet correctly.

◀**Inflatable rings** help you float with your feet off the pool bottom.

▶As you get better at swimming, you can try using a mask, **snorkel,** and flippers. You may not be allowed to use them at all pools.

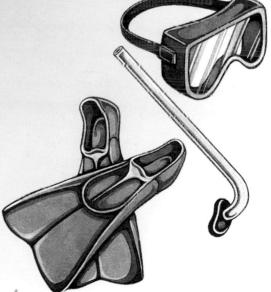

SAFETY STAR
Don't use a mask, snorkel, and flippers until you can swim well!

Is It Safe?

Make sure you swim only in a safe place.

Until you can swim well, only practice in water in which you can stand.

Never jump or dive into water until you know how deep and safe it is.

Never swim by yourself.

➤Read the pool or beach rules. Never run near a pool.

Don't swim in the ocean or a lake if warning flags are flying. Listen to the **lifeguards**. Never swim out too far. You might not be able to get back.

Think about the safety of other people, too.

Never jump or dive close to other people.

Never push people.

Never jump in if someone is in trouble or you could be in danger, too.

➤ If someone is in trouble in the water, throw them something that floats.

◄ Use something to pull the person to the side. He or she might be able to grab onto a pole, a T-shirt, or a towel.

Are You Ready?

Before you swim, make sure your body is ready by doing a **warm**-up. It helps you to swim better and keeps you from hurting yourself.

You must never run near a pool. But doing a short run somewhere nearby is a good way to warm up. You could run in place, too!

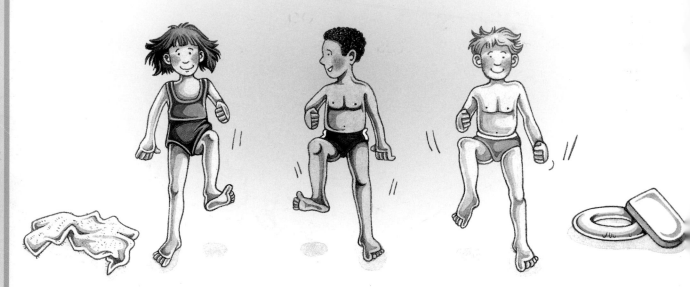

These exercises make your heart beat faster and make you breathe quicker. You will also feel warmer. All of these are good for your body to get it ready for a swim.

SAFETY STAR
Before you swim, you should do warm-up exercises.

You need to get your muscles warmed up.

The best way is to move all your **joints**. These are the parts of your body where you can bend, such as your shoulders, elbows, knees, and waist.

Try some **stretching** exercises, too. These make your muscles warmer and more stretchy.

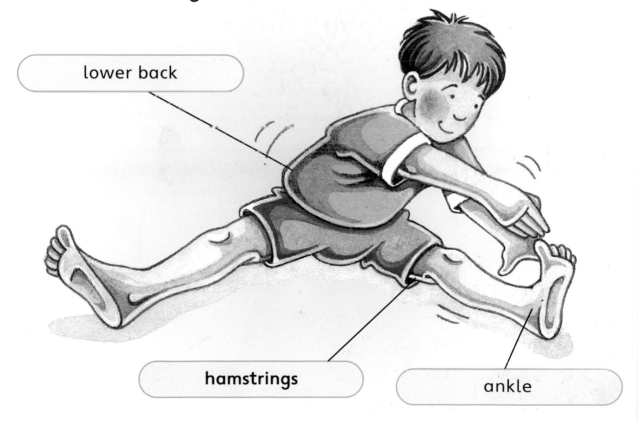

lower back

hamstrings

ankle

Now you are ready to get into the water.

Isn't Water Fun?

There are lots of ways to have fun while you learn to swim.

First you need to feel happy and safe in the water. Try walking around in the water to get used to it.

Next, try putting your whole body under the water.

Lower yourself so the water is just level with your mouth. Then lean forward and blow bubbles into the water. It's fun!

Now try putting your whole face under the water.

Take a deep breath before you put your head under. Then hold your breath and go under. Make sure you don't breathe in while you are underwater.

Can you open your eyes underwater? Try opening your eyes to count a partner's fingers.

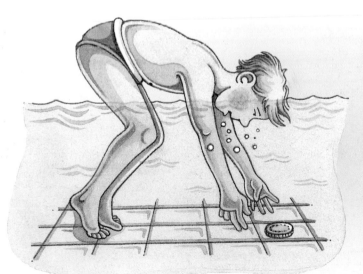

Drop something, such as a coin, to the bottom in shallow water. Now try to duck down and pick it up. Always have an adult watching when you do this.

More Things to Do

Once you can put your body under the water, you can try these things, too.

In shallow water, put your hands on the bottom and lift your legs up as far as you can. If you lift them high enough, they will float on the top. Then walk on your hands along the bottom of the pool.

Next put your face into the water as you go along. Lift your head up and down with each step you take with your hands.

Now you are ready to go into water that is a little deeper. At first use **water wings** or an **inflatable ring**.

Slowly walk from shallow water to deeper water. When your feet no longer touch the bottom, start to kick them so that they move you around.

Keep practicing. You should be able to move in all directions.

See if you can lift your feet higher and higher until they are kicking at the surface behind you. Now you can really move around.

Make Your Legs Work!

Get your legs working. Using your legs to move on your back is a great way to start. You can watch your legs and feet to make sure they are in the right place.

Put one **kickboard** under each arm. Begin by walking backwards. Then slowly lean back until you are lying flat in the water.

Now kick your legs and feet up and down, or move them in and out with a pushing movement, like a frog. Stay as flat as you can in the water.

Now you are ready to move onto your front.

Practice in shallow water. First, hold one end of a kickboard with two hands. Rest your arms on the board. Then lift your bottom and feet so you are flat in the water. Now kick your feet to push yourself along.

Next, hold the kickboard out in front of you with your arms straight. Try putting your head into the water and breathing out.

Moving on Your Front

Now practice swimming without a **kickboard**.
Make sure you are in shallow water.

The first **stroke** to learn is the dog paddle. Just kick with your legs and paddle with your hands! Try to make your body very flat as you move along.

To do the crawl, lift your arms up and over to pull yourself along. Try to put your head into the water and breathe out. This will make you flatter and you will move along better.

16

To do the breaststroke, make your hands flat and pull them in towards your face with your elbows up and out. Then push your hands away from you as far as you can. Spread your hands out to the side and pull them back.

To move forward, kick your legs like a frog as you move your arms. Your legs should be bent up toward your body at the same time that your hands are closest to your face.

Moving on Your Back

Some people find it easier to start by swimming on their backs. They can keep their faces out of the water and breathe more easily. Be careful. Don't bump your head on the side of the pool.

Start in shallow water. As you lean back, use your arms to keep you steady and straight.

The first **stroke** to learn on your back is called the elementary backstroke.

Lie flat on your back in a floating position. Do the same frog-leg kick you did for the breaststroke. Your arms should go beneath you and pull backward, just like someone rowing a boat!

If you turn your body to one side, you can do the sidestroke. Make long pulling movements with one arm. The other arm helps you keep your balance.

The backstroke is like the crawl, but you do it on your back. Remember, try to get your body flat in the water. This makes it easier for you to swim.

Jumping and Diving

Jumping into water is easy. Start in shallow water by crouching down and jumping off the side of the pool.

Once you are used to jumping in, you can go into water that is a bit deeper. Never jump into deep water unless you are a good swimmer. If you have a ring, use it as a target for your jump.

You can start diving when you are a good swimmer.

Sit at the edge of the pool with your knees tucked up. Put your hands together and your arms out straight in front of your head.

Then roll forwards into the water. Keep your chin on your chest and let your hands and arms go in first.

As you get used to this, you can move from sitting to crouching. Then slowly start your dive higher and higher until you can do it from a standing position. Never run and dive. You might slip.

◀Timing and balance are important for safe diving.

Keeping Safe

Swimming is great fun, but to be safe you should follow the safety tips in this book.

Every swimming pool and many beaches have rules. Read them and do what they say.

There may be areas at a beach or shore where swimmers are not allowed. Look for warning signs and flags. Always check with an adult to make sure that you are swimming in a safe place.

There usually are **lifeguards** at swimming pools and beaches. If you are not sure about any of the rules, ask a lifeguard.

Never go swimming unless there is an adult to look after you.

It is very dangerous to play foolishly. Never push other people into the water. Never hold anyone under the water.

Be very careful how you get into water. Before you jump or dive in, be sure it is safe to do so.

Don't go swimming right after you have eaten. Wait at least an hour or you may get pains in your stomach.

Keeping clean and safe

There are some other things you should know about swimming. They have to do with **hygiene**, which means keeping clean.

Don't swim in a public pool if you have a nose or an ear **infection**.

Always use the footbaths at the pool. They contain a special **chemical**. It helps to keep foot diseases from spreading to other people.

Take a quick shower before you get into the water. It is also a good idea to take a shower afterward, too, to wash off the chemicals from the pool water.

Use a clean towel to dry yourself. Make sure that all your swimming gear is washed often and kept clean.

Dry yourself carefully, especially between your toes.

Swimming is great fun, but you should always be very, very careful. Never take any risks, and remember,

YOU CAN DO IT!

Glossary

chemical substance put into water to make it clean

chlorine chemical that keeps pool water clean

earplugs small, plastic stoppers that keep water from getting into your ears

hamstring tendons at the back of the knee that connect leg muscles

hygiene rules for keeping clean and healthy

infection disease that can be passed to others

inflatable ring plastic ring filled with air to help you float in water

joint place on your body where bones meet and that can be bent

kickboard flat float used to stay up in the water

lifeguard person at pools and beaches who looks after swimmers

snorkel special tube that helps you breathe while your face is underwater

stretching moving your muscles at the joints as much as you can

stroke repeated swimming move of your arms and legs

warm-up exercises that get your body ready before swimming

water wings arm bands filled with air that help you float

Index

More Books to Read

Atkins, Jeannine. *Get Set! Swim!* New York: Lee & Low Books, Incorporated, 1998.

Bailey, Donna. *Swimming*. Austin, Tex.: Raintree Steck-Vaughn, 1990.

Loewen, Nancy. *Water Safety*. Chanhassen, Minn.: Child's World, 1996.